GUILDFORD
PAST & PRESENT

JOHN JANAWAY
AND
RON HEAD

COUNTRYSIDE BOOKS
NEWBURY

First Published 1985

© John Janaway 1985

COUNTRYSIDE BOOKS
3 CATHERINE ROAD
NEWBURY, BERKSHIRE

Designed and typeset by Publicity Plus, Newbury.
Produced through MRM (Print Consultants) Ltd., Reading.
Printed in England by J.W. Arrowsmith Ltd., Bristol.

ISBN 0 905392 54 X

INTRODUCTION

We are fortunate indeed that the last 120 years of change in Guildford have been so faithfully recorded by the town's many photographers. As a result, a large collection of photographs has survived for the Guildfordians of 1985 to compare and enjoy.

'The town of the golden ford' had grown up at the crossroads of several ancient routes, at a point where the river Wey had cut a narrow gap through the chalk of the North Downs and where, by a natural stroke of good fortune, the river was fordable. The town's wealth during the medieval period was based on the production of woollen cloth and the royal patronage of its substantial castle. Both had ceased to have any significance by the 17th century but, from this time, Guildford became increasingly important as the agricultural market and trading centre for a large area of West Surrey, a role which is still in the 1980s the basis for its prosperity. Also in the 17th century Portsmouth developed as the major naval centre, and the large number of travellers on the road between London and the port found Guildford an attractive resting place. The town's inns and alehouses became justly famous.

In 1845 the railway reached the town when the branch from Woking was opened. Of even more significance was the railway's subsequent extension to Godalming in 1849 and on to Havant and thus to Portsmouth in 1859. The coaching trade ceased abruptly and the town's hostelries started a decline in numbers which has continued to this day.

The railway brought new settlers, attracted by the character of the place and the ease of travel to London. Soon suburban villas began to ring the town and shopkeepers to replace innkeepers. The market also prospered, especially for corn and cattle, and in 1865, having outgrown the narrow confines of the High Street, it moved first to North Street and then, in 1895, to Woodbridge Road.

The response to the rising population and increasing affluence began to show all over Guildford. In North Street an impressive array of public buildings was erected. The ancient parish churches for various reasons became inadequate for the new parishioners — St Nicholas' was rebuilt in 1875 and Christchurch and St Saviour's were founded. Such growth was not confined to the Church of England, for Methodist, Congregationalist and Roman Catholic churches all took their place in the bustling panorama of an ancient town adjusting to an ever quickening pace of life.

In the High Street traders and shopkeepers came and went, but many stayed to become household names, still remembered by older Guildfordians — White's the drapers, Carling, Gill and Carling the ironmongers, Gammon's the drapers and Brett's Restaurants. Some have survived the onslaught of the large national retailers of the 20th century and are still with us, like Salsbury's the jewellers and Jeffery's, famed for sporting guns, fishing tackle and much else for more than 130 years.

Unfortunately, the attractions of Guildford as a retailing centre brought a huge volume of traffic to choke the streets. The response was gentle to begin with. As early as 1825 St Mary's Church in Quarry Street had been shortened to allow a freer flow of traffic and, in 1882, Onslow Bridge was opened, giving easier access to the railway station. In those days it was horse-drawn carts and wagons but, during the 1900s, the internal combustion engine began to make its appearance, and a problem which continues literally to consume the town had arrived. At first the destruction was slight, the widening of Ram Corner at the top of the High Street and the demolition of properties at the corner of Chertsey Street and North Street, for example.

In 1934 the Guildford and Godalming By-pass was opened but any improvements it brought seemed soon obscured. By the late 1950s the rapid increase in the number of car owners meant that something drastic needed to be done to alleviate the town's distress. When the answer arrived in 1972 in the shape of the 'gyratory' road system the response of most Guildfordians was justifiably mixed, to say the least. In 1985 it has hardly proved a success.

In the thirty years following the last war Guildford, in common with most commercially successful towns, was subjected to a rash of modern building, much of it totally out of scale with the varied and attractive jumble of previous centuries. The architect of the 19th century was also guilty of such misguided insertions, but time has often weathered their creations into acceptability and even enthusiastic appreciation in the 1980s. In contrast, the concrete of the post-war period does not mellow but soon becomes an eyesore through ugly staining and decay. However, several recent developments, for example in North Street and Chertsey Street, do give hope for a brighter future. In a thriving town some old buildings must give way to the new if the place is not to become a fossil. Let us hope that future building will always be in scale with the old, enough of which survives to continue to give this town its unique character.

We should like to thank the following for the loan of photographs or for information so helpfully given: Surrey Archaeological Society and Pat Ashworth, until recently their librarian; Surrey County Library Local Studies Library and staff members Mavis Davies, Duncan Mirylees, David Ryder and Doreen Williamson; Mrs Davies (nee Purnell), Reg Patrick, Chris Marks, Matthew Alexander, Thelma Ede, Janet Golden and last, but by no means least, our wives for help and encouragement at all times.

One late 19th century author said of Guildford: 'There is no southern county seat that looks its part better than Surrey's, even since in our day its time-honoured features have been much overlaid by new ones'. May this still remain true in the years to come.

JOHN JANAWAY
RON HEAD

CONTENTS

THE UNIQUE character of the town's High Street is well illustrated in this view. Until Farnham Road was built by the Turnpike Trust in 1758, the main road ran up The Mount and onto the Hogsback and thus to Farnham. In the other direction it was this sweep of road, across the river Wey via the Town Bridge and up the High Street towards London, which made Guildford a town of unrivalled character.

6

THE EXTENSION of Millbrook across the bottom of the High Street and the widening of Park Street have done much to destroy the view. The present St Nicolas Church was consecrated on 20th April 1876. It was originally intended to have a spire on top of the tower but this idea was abandoned because of the cost. Even the 'mini-spire' which was put up instead has now been removed.

GUILDFORD c. 1880

A VIEW of Guildford taken from the cemetery on The Mount. In the foreground is St Nicolas Church with the chimney of Lascelles, Tickner's Castle Brewery nearby. Further to the right can be seen the church of St Mary's with Holy Trinity beyond, whilst prominent on the far right is the Castle Keep.

TODAY THE iron railings and the neat hedge in the cemetery have gone and trees obscure much of the view. The Castle Brewery has been replaced by the CEGB offices but other landmarks remain. However, the scene is now dominated by the multi-storey car park in Sydenham Road and other modern developments.

A WAGON STANDS outside Robert Stone's shop on the corner of High Street and Portsmouth Road. Stone was a stationer, carver, gilder and picture-framer. The St Nicholas Church seen here was designed by Robert Ebbles and built in 1837 to replace the medieval church, which probably dated from the 13th century. The medieval tower was retained but plastered over and embellished.

EBBLES' CHURCH was never satisfactory and it was in a poor state of repair when demolished in 1875 to make way for the present church.

THE ENTRANCE to Park Street has changed beyond recognition. Even in 1900 it was so narrow that traffic was allowed along it only in one direction — the one-way system is nothing new to Guildford! The Barley Mow closed in 1906, becoming a bicycle shop and motor garage and finally an estate agents. The sign above the first floor of the pub advertised Crooke's Fine Stout and Porter which was brewed just a few yards away at The Guildford Brewery.

PARK STREET 1985

BY THE 1930s Stevenson's building had been demolished to improve the flow of traffic from High Street into Park Street. The cottages further up Park Street went in 1906 when the Technical Institute was built. Only the building in the distance, which until recently was an off-licence, is recognisable today.

13

PARK STREET & FARNHAM ROAD 1905

A MEMBER OF the Borough Constabulary stands guard at the junction of Park Street and Farnham Road. Traffic was obliged to 'keep to the left road' to reach the lower High Street, whilst traffic from the Portsmouth Road and High Street came up Park Street to Farnham Road. Guildford had its own independent police force until 1942.

14

OF THE BUILDINGS seen in 1905, only St Nicolas Church has survived the wholesale demolition of this area. The road where the wagon stood parked has disappeared beneath a car park and the much criticised 'gyratory' road system.

THE THREE Christ's Hospital boys are walking past a fine group of 16th and 17th century cottages, nos. 2 — 10 Farnham Road. They have no doubt just come to Guildford on the Horsham to Guildford Direct Railway, opened in 1865, which ran via Cranleigh and Bramley and was closed in 1965. On the far right can be seen the Farnham United Breweries' ale stores and off-licence.

THE FARNHAM ROAD cottages were demolished in 1957. An earlier attempt to have them removed in 1910 failed, but the ever increasing traffic which hurtled past their doors made them less desirable residences and their fate was sealed. One well known architectural authority said that 'they were the best of their type in the county and ought to have been preserved'. Their replacements are hardly up to the same standard.

FARNHAM ROAD 1911

THIS VIEW of Farnham Road was taken by a photographer from Francis Frith & Co. of Reigate, who were one of the leading postcard manufacturers of the day. It shows the Napoleon Hotel, originally called Napoleon III after Napoleon Bonaparte's nephew. Next door to the hotel was Miss Denton, stationer and registry office for servants; then came J. Belchamber, baker, W.F. Parnell, tobacconist and hairdresser, and then W.G. Heath, auctioneer, estate agent and surveyor.

HEATH'S STILL continue in this now devastated parade of shops as Heath & Salter. The Technical Institute, which could be seen in the distance in 1911 and later became the local education office, was demolished in 1972 to make way for the 'gyratory' traffic system. The trees are sadly missed from this now ugly scene.

19

LOWER HIGH STREET 1887

HENRY ALBERT HART was in business at 87 High Street as a fruiterer and greengrocer between 1887 and 1891. Next door at no. 88 was Christopher Wrist, grocer, pork butcher and coal merchant, who was Mayor of Guildford for three consecutive years in the 1890s. No. 86 looks shuttered and closed, as indeed it was — Wrist had been here up until 1886 before moving next door but one and his old premises remained empty until rebuilt in about 1891.

THE GREYHOUND INN and the two surviving shops now stand marooned and isolated from the main commercial core of the town, but surprisingly they are still officially in the High Street. From 1st January 1961 the High Street was renumbered using the odds and evens system and these premises became numbers 5 to 11.

ONE OF THE obvious dangers to the lower end of the town has always been that of flooding. This picture was taken during the disastrous flood of February 1900. On the afternoon of Thursday 15th February, the level of the river Wey rose dramatically when heavy rain followed a rapid thaw of snow, and in the early hours of Friday morning the river burst its banks. This photograph must have been taken on the morning of the 16th shortly before the Town Bridge collapsed.

22

THE EXTENSION of Millbrook now severs the lower High Street whilst work on the new Town Bridge, scheduled to be the original width but for pedestrians only, has just begun. The town last experienced serious flooding in September 1968 but, fortunately, later proposals for a drastic and disfiguring flood prevention scheme now appear to have been shelved.

TOWN BRIDGE c. 1870

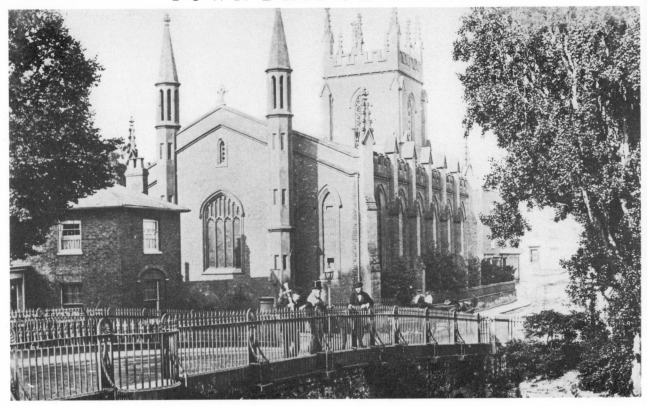

THE MEDIEVAL Town Bridge was much altered over the years. In 1763 the central arch, one of five, was widened to accommodate barges going up river to Godalming on the Godalming Navigation, a newly built extension to the Wey Navigation. In 1825 the bridge was repaired, widened and also acquired the iron railings seen in this photograph. The view is dominated by Robert Ebbles' church of 1837.

IN APRIL 1985 the stark lines of the St Nicolas Church of 1876 contrast sharply with the earlier church. Ebbles' church used the old medieval spire of the original building but the spire of the present church is at the opposite end nearer to the river. The house between the church and the river seems to have gone but may in fact be hidden behind later additions. In the foreground work has begun on the new Town Bridge.

25

TOWN BRIDGE 1900

BEMUSED AND BEHATTED the population of Guildford view their devastated bridge on 16th February 1900. The timber which swept down from Moon's yard is clearly seen. There would be much wrangling before the replacement bridge was opened in 1902. H. Martin, who ran the boathouse by the bridge, was also a confectioner and mineral water manufacturer. Opposite was F. Cobbett, basket maker, hence the partly visible 'Guildford Basket' sign on the wall.

THE TOWN BRIDGE of 1902 was demoted to a footbridge with the opening of the gyratory road system and finally condemned as unsafe. More baulks of timber now lie about the site as a new bridge begins to take shape. H. Martin's boathouse and shop, later Harry How's, was swept away by the Millbrook extension road and now an empty office towers coldly above the river scene. Also gone are all the premises opposite.

CROOKE'S BREWERY 1925

THE PHOTOGRAPHER stood by the side of the Town Bridge to take this view of the brewery of F.A. Crooke & Co. The Crooke family had been brewers in the town since the 18th century but this picture was taken in the very year, 1925, when the brewery was taken over by Hodgsons of Kingston. The Guildford Brewery or St Nicholas Brewery as it was known, was closed down in 1929.

CROOKE'S BREWERY 1985

ALL THE brewery buildings have been demolished and the area is now a car park. However, the modern scene is a pleasant one and it is hoped that plans to build a new museum on the site and to landscape the river bank will be successful. It is easy to come to the conclusion that Guildford is ashamed of its river and wishes to hide it away. Much more should be made of such a great asset.

THE TOWER of St Nicolas Church dominated the view of the river Wey from Onslow Bridge. The river towpath petered out in this stretch in the middle of the town and, during the commercial heyday of the navigation, barges would have been punted or poled upstream — undoubtedly a backbreaking task with a fully loaded craft against the current.

NOW THE NEW Friary Bridge, opened in 1972, cuts across the river and the church shares the skyline with an office block. However, an admirable development on the bank in the far left has preserved and extended a view of some character.

FRIARY STREET 1900

THE WATERS rise in Friary Street in February 1900. The group standing outside C. Roberts' clothing and furniture store are more concerned with posing for the camera than avoiding getting their feet wet. Next door to Roberts was Fletcher the butcher, followed by J. Staerck, fruiterer, and then The Bear Inn, whose cellars must have been well filled with flood water by the time this picture was taken.

FRIARY STREET was redeveloped and then opened for pedestrians only in 1972. It was hoped to save The Bear and the adjacent property but, in the event, only the facades were saved — incongruous companions to the harsh and insensitive lines of the supermarket opposite.

PERRIDGE'S Old Blue China Shop of 104 High Street and 67 Quarry Street became the High Street branch of W.H. Smith's in 1929. For most of the 19th century The Star Inn was run by Jesse Boxall. There were three generations of them. Jesse I leased the pub in 1792 and ran it until the 1830s when his son, Jesse II took over. Jesse III bought the premises in 1845 and was landlord until his death in 1894.

THE JUNCTION of High Street and Quarry Street seen in the previous picture in 1928 has changed little to this day. Now marred, perhaps, by a plethora of traffic signs and bollards. The present firm of Cubitt and West occupies premises which have housed an estate agent and auctioneer for over 60 years. In the distance Guildford's oldest church, St Mary's, is almost hidden. The Star flourishes and is still as popular as it was in the days of the Boxalls.

35

THE YOUNG LADY with the pram stands outside Thomas Hampton's shop, 53 Quarry Street, on the corner of Castle Street. Hampton was one of several antique furniture dealers already established in the town by this time. Guildford became quite well known for its antique and reproduction furniture, although whether the latter was always sold as such can only be surmised.

THE TREES in St Mary's churchyard have gone to be replaced, thankfully, by others. How important it is to have trees within a town, a point so often lost in modern developments. Fortunately, this end of Quarry Street has not suffered the indignities inflicted upon other parts of Guildford, although the boarded up state of No. 53 does leave some cause for concern and at least one other building here is under threat at the present time.

QUARRY STREET c. 1870

MANY OF THE buildings in Quarry Street have character both front and back. Their owners had a fine view of the river to appreciate and gardens which led right down to the millstream. Several of the properties acquired large bay windows from which the residents could admire the prospect.

THE CONSTRUCTION of Millbrook to relieve the traffic congestion in Quarry Street destroyed this relative tranquility, whilst the construction of various intensive modern extensions has done little to help the view.

HIGH STREET c.1885

A TRANQUIL High Street on a sunny day can now only be appreciated early on a Sunday morning before the ubiquitous motorists have left their beds. All is quiet on the sunny side of the street in about 1885, where the awnings are out to shade the window displays of drapers, outfitters, china dealers, confectioners, corset makers and the like. The building in the left foreground was The Bridge House Hotel which closed in 1928.

40

HIGH STREET 1985

UNFORTUNATELY, the modern shopper arrives by car and requires new roads and car parks, much to the detriment visually of the town. Pedestrians must now be fenced in like football fans to prevent them from impeding the fast flow of traffic into, and occasionally out of, the 'gyratory' road system. The Bridge House Hotel later became a ladies' costumiers and was finally demolished in 1971 to make way for the new road.

HIGH STREET 1878

FRANK LASHAM took over the stationer, printer and publisher business of Andrews & Son in 1878. Is it the proud new owner standing in the doorway of his High Street premises in this photograph taken in that year? Lasham's major contribution to the town was the publication of the *Almanac and Directory* which Biddles continued to publish under his name until 1935. Next to Lasham's, Wood's clothier store became Wood, White and Tucker in 1877, later White and Tucker and, by the 1900s, W.E. White.

HIGH STREET 1985

LASHAM'S IS now Randall's shoe shop, much altered and showing how difficult it is to sort out genuine fronts from modern mocks in a High Street with a fair share of both. The famous firm of 'White's', which also had a branch in North Street, continued in business in the High Street until 1959. Marks & Spencer opened here after much rebuilding in July 1962.

THE IMPORTANCE of Guildford as the commercial and trading centre of a large area of West Surrey can be readily appreciated in both these pictures, taken 82 years apart. In 1903 the High Street bustles with carts, carriages and wagons. On the right-hand side of the street the lamp hangs outside the premises of Nealds and Cooper, wine and spirit merchants, who were established in the town in 1775 and ceased trading soon after the First World War.

HIGH STREET 1985

ON A SATURDAY in 1985 carts and carriages have been replaced by hundreds of shoppers now free to walk at leisure in the middle of the road. This is a much happier situation than 80 years ago when accidents between walkers and wheels were not inknown. When the motor car first appeared on the town's streets the accident rate rose alarmingly, especially those involving children who had previously been used to wandering carelessly in the road.

HIGH STREET c. 1900

R. SALSBURY OPENED his High Street watchmaking and jewellery business in 1870 having taken over from Busby and Baxter, who had been watchmakers here since the 1840s. A business guide published in 1892 said of Salsbury's that 'this old-established business has since its earliest career enjoyed a reputation for the superiority of goods sold and the moderation of prices charged'. Like many other traders of his generation, Salsbury involved himself in local politics, being mayor in 1894 and 1895.

HIGH STREET 1985

SALSBURY'S CONTINUE in business in the same premises in 1985, having also expanded next door. W.J. Nunn was a tailor and hatter and this shop later became The Astolat Tea Rooms and School of Cookery under the guidance of Miss Edith Gillam. By the 1930s it had been divided into a hairdresser's and a tobacconist's. This fine 17th century building has altered little over the years.

SWAN LANE c. 1930

SWAN LANE, like Market Street which was once known as Red Lion Gate, developed from the entrance and yard of one of Guildford's famous coaching inns. Angel Gate has survived as a reminder of the town's heyday as the mecca of travellers on the Portsmouth Road before the coming of the railways. In the spring of 1930 Ye Olde Swanne Restaurant served dinners and teas where once mutton chops and claret were the order of the day. The building is thought to have once been part of The Swan Inn.

SWAN LANE 1985

IN 1931 Ye Olde Swanne Restaurant closed but in 1960 the gastronomic connection was revived and in 1965 it became The Mermaid Restaurant. Unfortunately, in 1985 it is once more a memory. Many Guildfordians will also have fond recollections of visits to the 'Dolls Hospital' which very sadly closed down quite recently. The spire of the Methodist Church in North Street, prominent above the rooftops in 1930, disappeared in 1973 when the church was demolished.

BRETT AND SON, cooks confectioners and caterers, established in Guildford before 1853, had two branches in the High Street by 1892. During the 1900s they traded as Brett, Reynard and Co. with an additional branch in Stoke Road. From 1912 they were simply known as Bretts, with their main restaurant at 108 High Street. In 1922 their advertisements claimed that it was 'Surrey's premier social rendezvous and the mecca of visitors to Guildford and West Surrey'.

50

THE 108 HIGH STREET premises was taken over in 1927 by Woolworths, who remained there until moving across the road in 1958 into a vast new shop (now demolished) built on the site of the Lion Hotel. W.H. Smith had moved into the High Street on the corner of Quarry Street in 1929, having run the bookstall on the railway station for many years. Quite recently they moved just a few yards up the street to no. 56, being the re-numbered 108 High Street.

THE GUILDHALL with its clock is undoubtedly the town's most famous landmark. Almost as well known is The Bull's Head, a rare survivor of Guildford's once numerous High Street public houses. During the 19th century the choice of pubs was enormous. For example, The Red Lion is just visible on the left, the premises of Peak and Lunn, architects, had previously been The George and Dragon whilst next door and almost under the Guildhall clock was The Guildford Arms.

52

IT WAS THE coming of the railway in 1845 which began the decline of the town's hostelries, a process which has continued to this day with the most recent closure being The Little White Lion in North Street. On a happier note The Black Friars has opened at the Friary Centre. Since the last war there have been two attempts to close The Bull's Head, the more recent attempt will still be fresh in the minds of most Guildfordians.

53

MENTION HAS ALREADY been made of the many fine public houses and inns in the High Street which are now closed. The same process has also continued in the back streets too. On the corner of Castle Street and Chapel Street was The Rose and Crown, which closed down in 1916. Opposite was The Elephant and Castle, which also shut in 1916, serving ales from Hodgson's Kingston Brewery.

54

THE ELEPHANT AND CASTLE has been demolished but its replacement has much charm, avoiding as it does grey slabs of concrete and plate glass. The Rose and Crown is now occupied by Singer Sewing Machines, a firm which has long connections with the town and, until recently, was based in the upper High Street.

CASTLE STREET c. 1912

THE TWO BREWERS in Castle Street is a pub of much character which is happily still with us. In 1912 it was tied to the Farnham United Breweries who were later taken over by Courages. Mrs Dean was the landlady. The archway to the right was the back entrance to Read & Co.'s butchers shop in the High Street. 'Fine pickled tongues' were one of their advertised specialities.

IN 1985 IT IS 2.15 p.m. on an April Sunday afternoon and many happy customers are heading for a late lunch. Further down Castle Street other cottages have been rebuilt but in a style wholly in keeping with the setting. It is a pity that this example has not been followed throughout the rest of Guildford. Once again the ubiquitous motorcar is much in evidence.

THE QUEENS HEAD was a quaint tile-hung pub in South Street which closed down in 1914. It later housed The Castle Press of Stent & Co., printers. Just beyond the 'good cycle stores' sign was the entrance to Milkhouse Gate. The name South Street disappeared in the early 1960s when it became part of Sydenham Road.

BUT, OH DEAR! That charming group of cottages was swept away for the worst piece of architecture in the town — the Sydenham Road multi-storey car park. There is little that can be said in favour of such an insensitive building — the modern photograph speaks for itself.

HIGH STREET c. 1870

AT ONE TIME the ground floor of the Guildhall was open and used as an overflow for the Cornmarket opposite. Later it housed one of the town's three fire engines. In 1870 the building adjacent was George Holden's Boot and Shoe Warehouse whilst next door was Shepherd the chemist. At Shepherd's Mr. Alex, surgeon dentist from London, attended every Monday for the 'painless' extraction of the inhabitants' teeth.

HIGH STREET 1985

SHEPHERD'S PREMISES were rebuilt soon after 1870, only to be demolished again in 1884 along with Holden's Boot and Shoe Warehouse and the Town Hall Hairdressing Salon upstairs. The London and County Bank, now the National Westminster Bank, was erected on the site. The council met at the Guildhall until new offices were opened in the upper High Street in 1931 but now the affairs of the much enlarged borough council have been transferred to new offices in Millmead.

TUNSGATE c. 1912

THE ORIGINAL Tuns Inn had stood in the High Street and was demolished in 1818 for the new Cornmarket but the name Tunsgate has survived to this day. The gentleman standing at the door of The Three Tuns in Tunsgate may be W. Boozer himself. Mr. Boozer was here from 1909 to 1915, having previously been landlord of the Bridge House Hotel near the town bridge. His appropriate name is, of course, much older than the American slang for drink.

THE CORNMARKET was moved to Woodbridge Road in 1901 but fortunately proposals to demolish the old Cornmarket with its imposing columned entrance fronting the High Street, were defeated. The old courthouse at the rear was removed and, during the latter part of 1936 and early 1937, the two central columns were moved further apart to provide access to a car park. This was situated on the site of the present Tunsgate Square development.

HOLY TRINITY CHURCH PRE 1888

WHILST THE medieval church of Holy Trinity was undergoing repairs and restoration in 1740, the tower collapsed through the roof. For two years the ruin lay undisturbed and it was another seven years before the foundation stone of the new church was laid. Building proceeded slowly but eventually in 1763 the new church was consecrated.

THE EXTENSION to the church which now obscures the buildings in the High Street including the chimneys of Abbot's Hospital, dates from 1888. In 1927 the Diocese of Guildford was created and, until the building of the Cathedral on Stag Hill, Holy Trinity served as the cathedral church.

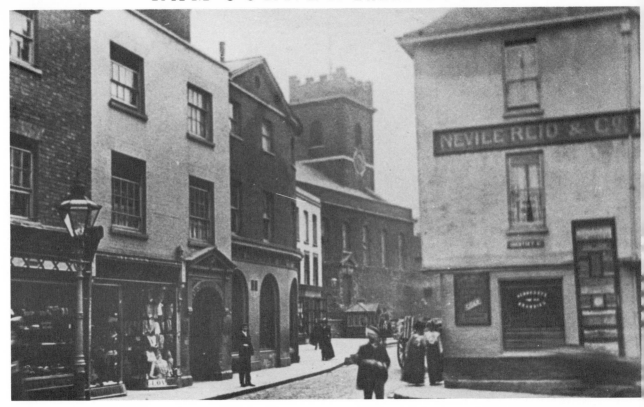

RAM CORNER was considered by one newspaper in 1912 as 'undoubtedly the worst point on the South Coast main roads'. The High Street narrowed to only 13 feet at the top of the hill. It is difficult to imagine the modern traffic of Guildford coping with such an obstacle. On the far left in this photograph, behind the lamp standard, was Brett, Reynard & Co's upper High Street restaurant, whilst next door was the millinery and fancy draper's business of A.E. Steer.

THE RAM INN was predictably demolished for road widening in 1913 but proposals to landscape the part of the site not used for the road were dashed when the land was sold to Barclays Bank. Beyond the Constitutional Hall, the imposing archways of the London, City and Midland Bank have gone, although the 'Midland' still occupies the site. Steer's premises and the hall next door were taken over by Thomas Thorp before the Second World War.

A GROCER'S delivery van stands parked in upper High Street. It almost certainly belongs to Tyler's grocers and wine merchants shop seen on the far left. Next door was Morton's Boot and Shoe Stores, whilst opposite stands Somerset House, a fine Queen Anne town house, built as a resting place for the Duke of Somerset on his travels between London and his country estates at Petworth. This end of the High Street was called Spital Street until 1901.

SOMERSET HOUSE still survives, although disfigured by shop fronts, but all the properties on the north side of the street have been demolished. The gas lamp has gone, to be replaced by the ubiquitous 'no waiting' sign. Guildford's gas company was founded in 1824 and it was not until 1930 that the last gas lamp was removed, leaving the borough's streets entirely lit by electricity.

THIS VIEW of a varied group of 17th century cottages and workshops was taken between 1896 and 1903. The aproned lady standing at the entrance to Cook's Passage may be Mrs Wapshott, who lived there at that time. This passage was one of many alleyways all over the town which led to small groups of crowded tenements behind the street frontage. The cart stands outside the wheelwright and coach builders business of Messrs. Carpenter & Thompson.

THE PREMISES of G.C. Pond, dyer, cleaner and carpet beater were demolished in 1904 to make way for an extension to the Working Men's Home and Coffee Tavern, which opened here in 1896. This view is taken from a position further up Chertsey Street in order to show the whole of the Home, now the Church Army Hostel. The cottages were demolished in 1933 for a further extension to the Home and also a car park. The wheelwright's shop was removed in 1937.

CHERTSEY STREET c. 1910

IN THE EARLY 1850s Cardinal Wiseman bought a piece of land and a beerhouse known as The Bars in Chertsey Street as the site for a Catholic church. In 1860 an ex-army wooden hut from Aldershot was erected by Catholic soldiers from the barracks under Captain Tredcroft. The beerhouse closed in 1863 and became the priest's house. Eventually on 19th October 1881 the foundation stone of St Joseph's church was laid.

ST JOSEPH'S church opened on 19th August 1884 and served the many Catholics of Guildford for almost 100 years. The new church in Eastgate Gardens, which was completed in the autumn of 1984, is a fine modern building. Also the replacement building in Chertsey Street is proof that modern architects are at last beginning to produce buildings which are human in scale.

73

CHERTSEY STREET PRE 1916

ONE OF GUILDFORD'S ancient pubs which fell foul of the local highways committee was the Dolphin Inn in Chertsey Street. In 1916 the committee was set on improving the flow of traffic on the corner of Chertsey Street and North Street and the building came down despite much local and even national protest.

CHERTSEY STREET 1985

THE OLD DOLPHIN INN was a short way down from the junction of the two streets with a yard which ran right through to North Street. It was re-built of brick on the corner of the two streets and in turn was removed to make way for Dolphin House in 1964. This new building was so vital to Guildford's economy that it remained empty for six years until Habitat came to the town in 1972.

ANOTHER BOTTLENECK for town traffic was the narrow bend at the top of North Street where the Crown Inn jutted out into the thoroughfare. The building was erected in 1728 as the Poorhouse for the paupers of the town's three parishes but it was sold at auction in 1837 and became an inn soon after. The Crown closed in 1906 and was demolished the following year.

GEORGE ABBOT'S Cloth Hall next door to the Crown was built in 1629 as part of an unsuccessful scheme to revive the town's failing cloth industry. It was a school until after the last war. The Job Centre now occupies the site where Bramwell & Co., egg importers and wholesale fruit merchants, were based. Bramwell's closed down in 1906. In the background in 1985 Maples furniture store, once a classic example of modern stained concrete has recently received a welcome facelift.

THE FIRE STATION. The Engine House was opened in February 1872 on the site of a wooden shed, which had been used to house one of the town's three fire engines since 1833. The architect of the fine new building was Henry Peak, borough surveyor and later mayor in 1899. His plans here included a tall bell tower but the ever thrifty council economised on its height. Consequently the sounding of the fire warning bell was inaudible over a large part of the town!

IN 1937, THE PRESENT fire station in Ladymead was opened and the North Street premises were converted to a public convenience. A fine clock with black and gold faces, which was given by the mayor Alderman Trigg in 1873, has been replaced by a much more mundane example. Next door the Horse and Groom, scene of the terrible bombing in 1974, continues as a popular survivor of the once numerous North Street pubs.

WITH SO MANY pubs, beerhouses, inns and beershops in the town it was not surprising that, as a reaction, the temperance movement gained a strong following. On 4th August 1880, the Earl of Onslow laid the foundation stone for The Royal Arms Coffee Tavern and Temperance Hotel. The ceremony was conducted with much 'earnestness', commented the *Surrey Advertiser* and the children of various Bands of Hope paraded the town.

80

IN 1892 the Guildford and Working Men's Institute was built adjacent to the Coffee Tavern in Ward Street. The work was done in exactly the same style as the Tavern, which opened in 1881, and today gives all the appearance of being part of the original building. The Guildford Institute had become somewhat moribund by the 1960s but has now come under the wing of Surrey University. Once again it plays a major part in both the education and relaxation of many Guildfordians. 81

IN 1800 A MARKET for meat, poultry, fish, butter, eggs, fruit and vegetables was established in the disused cockpit in Red Lion Yard. In 1818 this market expanded to include the recently vacated courthouse. It was not long before the whole of the Red Lion Yard was taken up with stalls on market days and the yard thus became known as Market Street. The 'green' market moved to North Street in 1887 and then to Woodbridge Road in 1896.

82

THE PRESENT MARKET in North Street, which is almost entirely fruit, vegetables and flowers, was not re-established at its now familiar site until after the First World War. In 1921 the stalls faced out onto the street but the ever increasing volume of traffic has driven shoppers onto the overcrowded haven of a narrow pavement. However, the tradition of friendly service from stallholders has continued to this day.

83

THE GAMMON BROTHERS, Ebenezer and James, who were born in Petersfield, had a draper's shop in Godalming by 1867. Their business flourished and branches were established at Farncombe and Haslemere. In 1878 James opened premises in North Street, Guildford.

THE SHOP SEEN here was built in 1895 and is yet another Henry Peak design. Since the photograph of the 1920s it has survived relatively unscathed apart from the removal of the pediments and chimneys. Gammons sold out to Debenhams in about 1962 and were closed down in 1967, yet another example of a local firm giving way to a national chain.

NORTH STREET boasted a fine array of public buildings. They were built in the 19th century mostly of Bargate stone. The stone dressings were of Bath stone. In the left foreground the Post Office was the exception, being constructed mainly of brick in 1886. Next up the street came the Congregational Hall of 1884 and then the Congregational Church built in 1863. Beyond the junction of Leapale Road was the County and Borough Halls.

ALL HAVE NOW vanished from the scene. The old Post Office was demolished in 1971 and, although the present Post Office building has been much criticised, at least it is not an overgrown slab of stained concrete. The Congregational Church and Hall were demolished in 1965 and replaced by an unsympathetic building. Part of the County and Borough Halls became the Guildford Theatre and was later incorporated in the Co-op, to be finally demolished recently.

THE SURREY Militia Barracks were built at the bottom of North Street in 1854 by the Earl of Lovelace, much in the same style of architecture which he used on his estates. In this case the barracks were of Bargate stone rather than the flint and brick of his many properties in East Horsley and Ockham. These barracks were the depot for the Militia until 1876, and then used by various corps of the Surrey Rifle Volunteers until about 1889.

DENNIS BROS. acquired the barracks for their rapidly expanding business in 1900 but, in less than a year plans were made to build their own premises on the corner of Onslow Street and Bridge Street. Soon these also proved inadequate and in 1905 they moved to Woodbridge Hill. Later part of the Militia Barracks housed Coombs Garage but this quaint Victorian structure, with its archway adding a Toytown atmosphere to this part of Guildford, was demolished in 1970.   89

BEDFORD ROAD 1919

IN 1905 THE Brighton mineral water manufacturers, Shelvey, opened a branch in Onslow Street. Shelveys continued in business at Guildford until 1918 when their manager, Edgar Purnell, took over in his own name and moved to Bedford Road. Both Edgar Purnell, who came originally from Shoreham, and his excellent products are still remembered by many of the older inhabitants of Guildford. Purnells were one of the last firms in the country to sell their ginger beer in stoneware bottle — the last of these bottle being supplied to them by Bournes of Denby in 1949.

BEDFORD ROAD 1985

PURNELLS MOVED to Bury Fields in 1927 and later to Stoke Road. They were eventually taken over by another Brighton firm, R. Fry & Co., and ceased production in 1952. The Weyside Mineral Water Works still stands and is now used as auction rooms by Clarke, Gammon. This firm was first established in the town in the early 1920s as Clarke, Gammon and Bullen, later Clarke, Gammon and Emerys.

ARTINGTON & GUILDOWN c. 1870

THIS VIEW OF Artington was taken from St Catherine's Hill. The villa residences of the prosperous and expanding middle class of Guildford climb the south facing hill above the ancient hamlet and the Portsmouth Road. Booker's Tower is prominent on the top of the hill. It was built in 1839 by Charles Booker as a memorial to his two sons, who both died in their youth.

92

IT IS NOW impossible to stand on St Catherine's Hill and see the view from the same position. Trees now obscure it almost completely. In the countryside of Surrey in 1985 there are undoubtedly many more trees than there were 100 years ago. Many of these have grown up in the gardens of the middle class villas. And on the top of the hill Booker's Tower, once a famous Guildford landmark, is now visible only during the winter months when the trees are bare.

FERRY LANE 1909

FERRY LANE, St Catherine's. The lane led down to the St Catherine's Ferry where walkers were punted across the river Wey. This was part of the ancient trackway romantically named 'The Pilgrims' Way' by the Victorians. In fact, this route for travellers of all descriptions was here long before the occasional pilgrim ever set foot on it.

NOW THE LANE has been moved to the right of the line of trees and the cottages have acquired gardens where it once ran. The ferry closed just over 20 years ago, necessitating a major detour, but now a recently opened footbridge has restored the ancient route.

OTHER SURREY TITLES AVAILABLE FROM COUNTRYSIDE BOOKS

The Surrey Village Book   *Graham Collyer*
Surrey: A Photographic Record   *John Janaway*
Tales of Old Surrey   *Matthew Alexander*
The Story of Godalming   *John Janaway*

For a complete catalogue of our publications please write to:

Countryside Books
3 Catherine Road
Newbury
Berkshire RG14 7NA